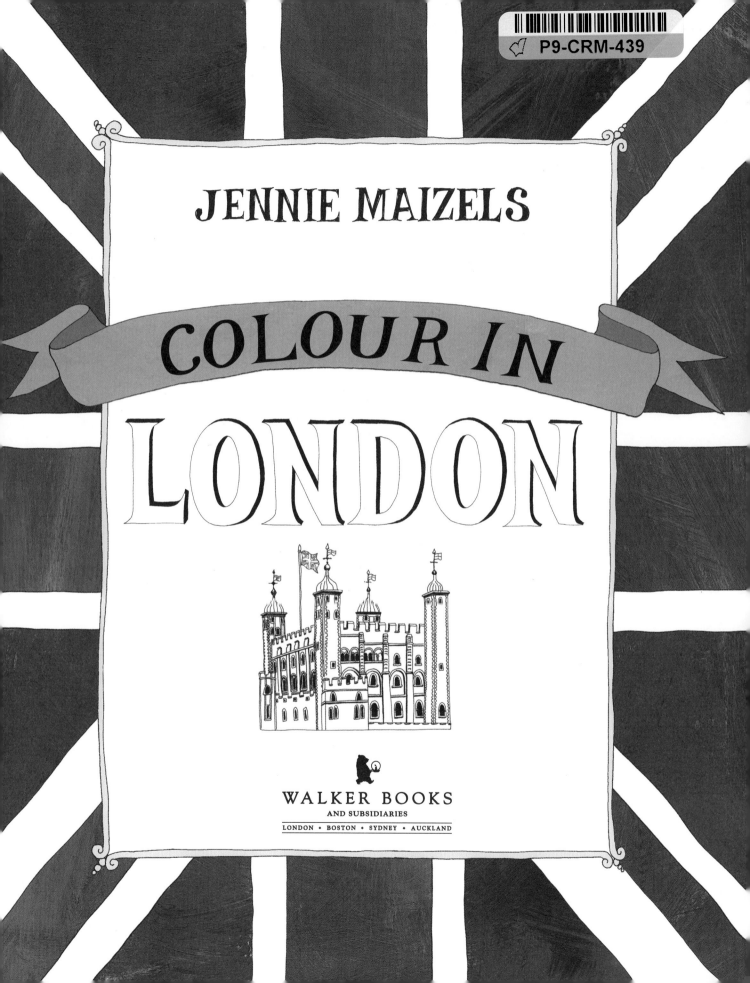

JENNIE MAIZELS

COLOUR IN

LONDON

WALKER BOOKS

AND SUBSIDIARIES

LONDON · BOSTON · SYDNEY · AUCKLAND

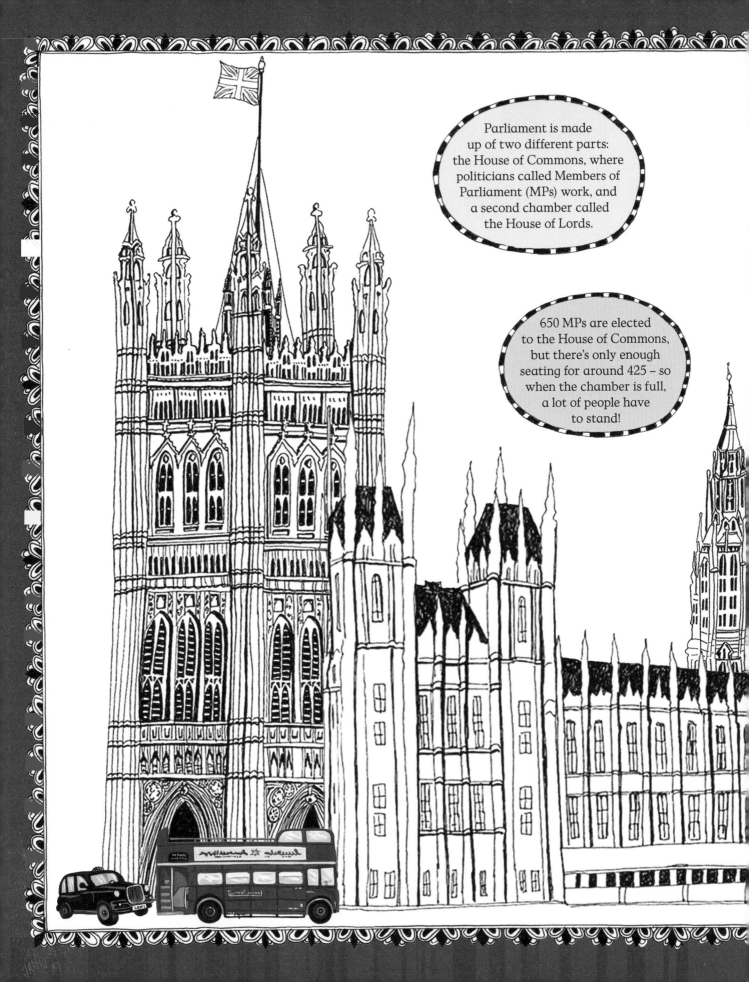

Parliament is made up of two different parts: the House of Commons, where politicians called Members of Parliament (MPs) work, and a second chamber called the House of Lords.

650 MPs are elected to the House of Commons, but there's only enough seating for around 425 – so when the chamber is full, a lot of people have to stand!

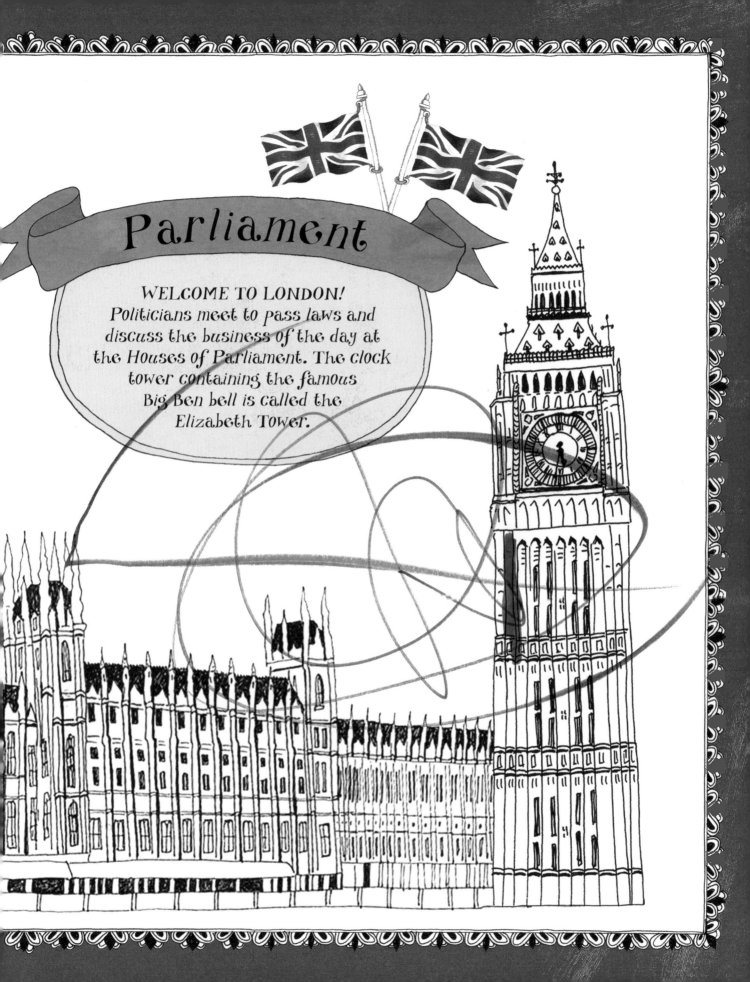

Parliament

WELCOME TO LONDON!
Politicians meet to pass laws and discuss the business of the day at the Houses of Parliament. The clock tower containing the famous Big Ben bell is called the Elizabeth Tower.

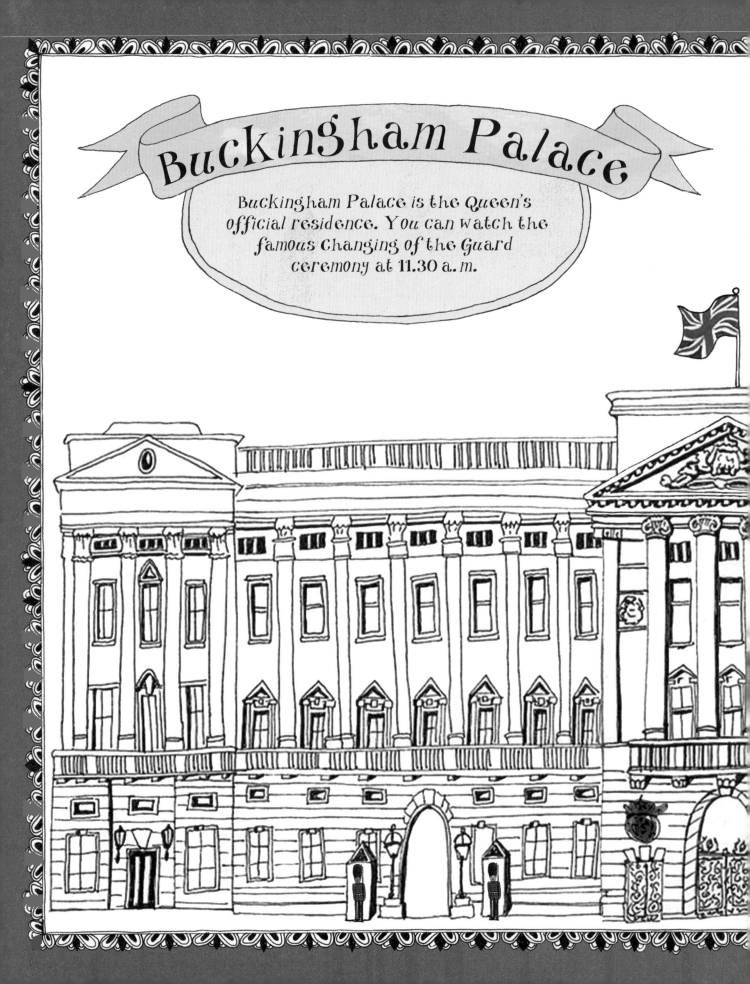

Buckingham Palace

Buckingham Palace is the Queen's official residence. You can watch the famous Changing of the Guard ceremony at 11.30 a.m.

A flag always flies above the palace. When the Queen is in residence, the Royal Standard flies. When she's away, the Union Jack is hoisted instead.

Colour in the Union Jack.

Tate Modern

Tate Modern is Britain's most important modern art gallery. The building was originally a power station.

This type of art is called drip painting. Try some at home!

Rare peregrine falcons live in the tower of the Tate Modern.

The most famous display area is Turbine Hall, which once housed electricity generators. Now it features large pieces of art specially designed for the space.

Shakespeare's Globe

The *Globe* is a reconstruction of the theatre that presented many of William Shakespeare's plays in Elizabethan times. The original *Globe* was closed in 1642.

Alas, poor Yorick!

Shakespeare's Globe received special permission to have a thatched roof – there has been a law against thatched buildings in London since the Great Fire in 1666 destroyed many thousands of homes.

Westminster Abbey

Westminster Abbey is almost 800 years old. Royal coronations are conducted there, and seventeen previous monarchs rest in its grounds.

Create your own colourful stained-glass window!

Each of Westminster Abbey's four cloisters is about 30 metres long. You can visit them for free!

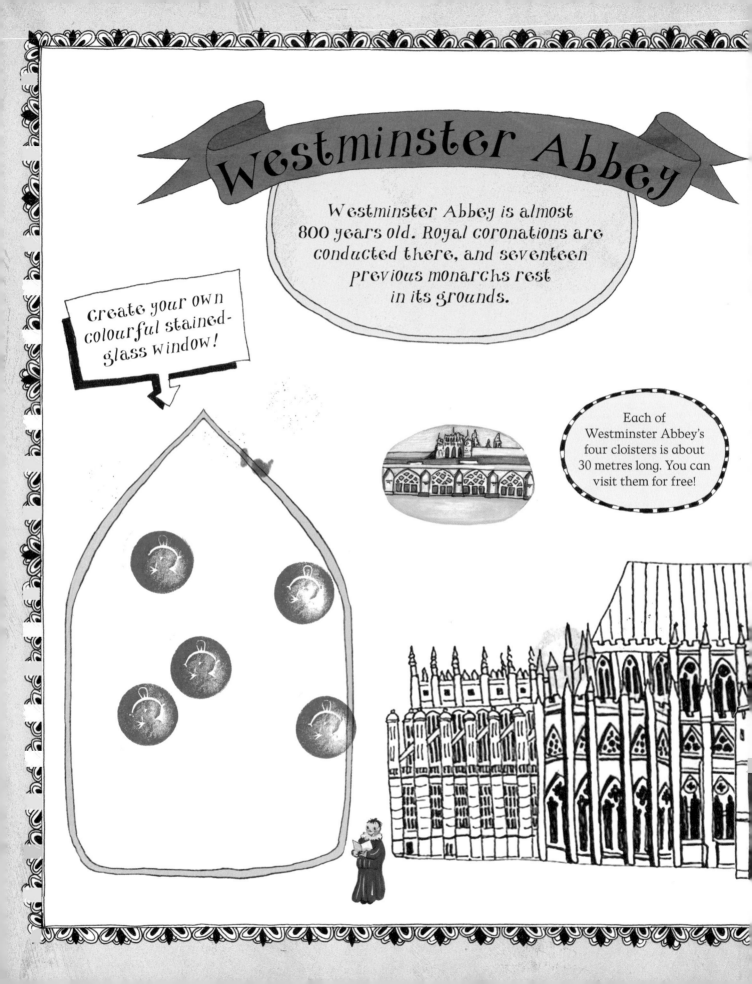

Prince William and Catherine Middleton married at Westminster Abbey in April 2011.

10 Downing Street

The British Prime Minister has been based at Number 10 since the house was presented to Robert Walpole, the first Prime Minister, by King George II.

The street is named after George Downing, the diplomat who built it. He used cheap construction materials to save money – after 200 years of improvements, 10 Downing St was still called "shaky and lightly built" by Winston Churchill!

I don't have keys to my house! But there's always someone to let me in.

Trafalgar Square

At the centre of Trafalgar Square is Nelson's Column, commemorating the victor of the Battle of Trafalgar. The square often hosts national celebrations and political demonstrations.

When the square was built, funds ran out before a statue could be mounted on the final plinth. After standing empty for centuries, it now displays contemporary artworks.

Draw your own monument on the Fourth Plinth.

Hamleys

Hamleys is the world's oldest toy shop, and one of the very biggest. Over 50,000 toys fill its shelves on seven different floors!

Father Christmas visits Hamleys every year to tell Christmas stories, sing songs and meet children.

Hamleys was bombed five times in World War Two, but stayed open – staff took orders at the entrance, then dashed into the shop wearing tin hats to collect the toys.

What toy would you buy?

TOYS HAMLEYS TOYS

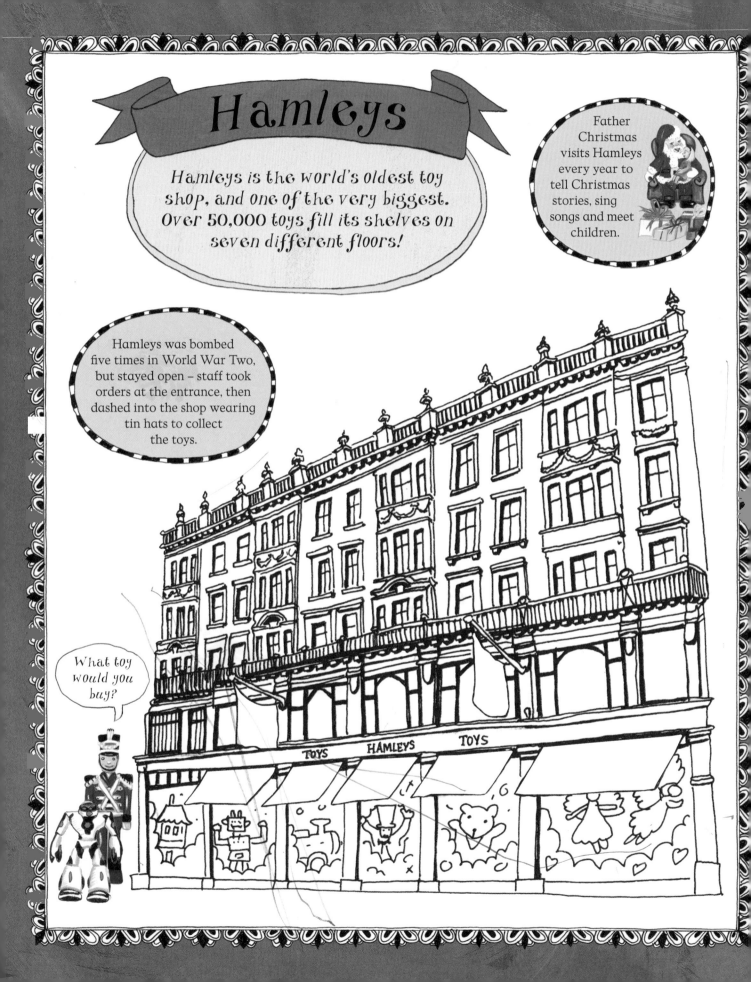

Kew Gardens

Kew Gardens has its own police force, Kew Constabulary, which has patrolled the grounds since 1947. Its officers act more as park rangers than as enforcers of the law!

Royal Botanic Gardens, Kew is home to the world's largest collection of living plants – more than 30,000 types! It also has over seven million preserved plants.

Follow this colour key to complete the picture.

Harrods

Harrods is the biggest department store in Europe. Located in upmarket Knightsbridge, it is famous for selling expensive items.

Harrods hired a live Egyptian cobra to protect the shoe counter in 2007, guarding a pair of jewel-encrusted shoes worth £62,000!

In 1898, Harrods opened Britain's first "moving staircase", now known as an escalator. Anxious customers were offered brandy at the top to help them recover!

Draw your own window display!

Natural History Museum

The Natural History Museum is jam-packed with amazing exhibitions. Feel the ground shake in the earthquake simulator, steer clear of T. rex's teeth and marvel at the huge blue whale model!

Natural history was once a department of the British Museum, but its collection got so big that it soon needed a building all to itself: the Natural History Museum!

Finish the dinosaur drawings, then colour them in.

St Paul's Cathedral

For more than 1,400 years, a cathedral dedicated to St Paul has stood here. The current building was built in the 1600s. Its famous dome is recognized worldwide.

Inside the dome is the mysterious Whispering Gallery. A whisper on one side can be heard clearly on the other, over 30 metres away!

I'm the Bishop of London.

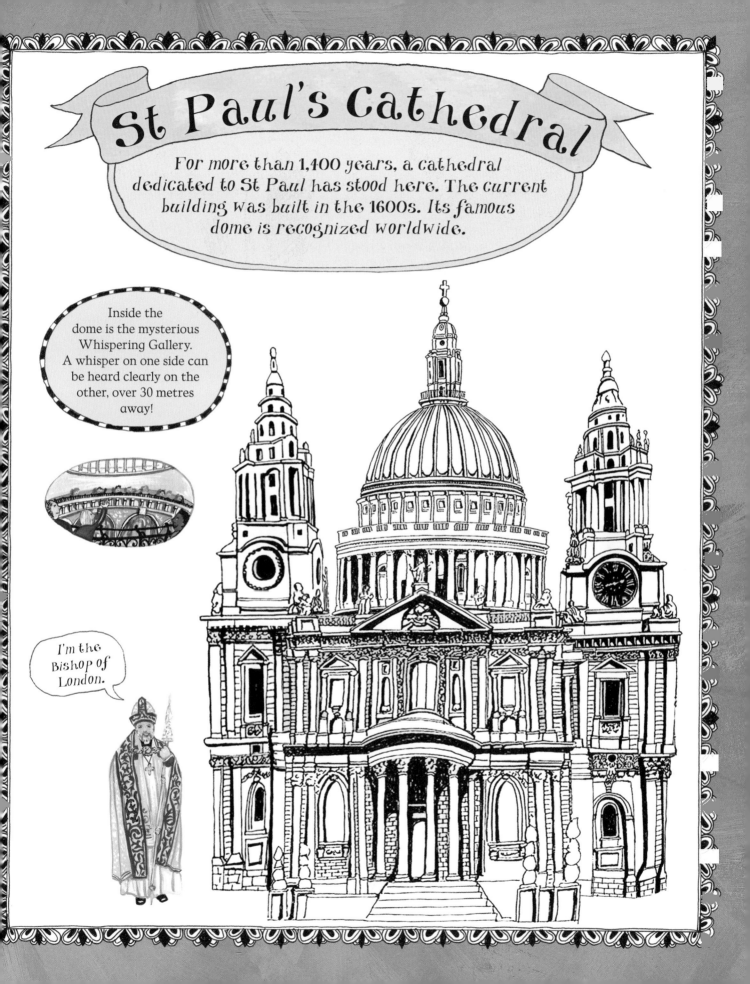

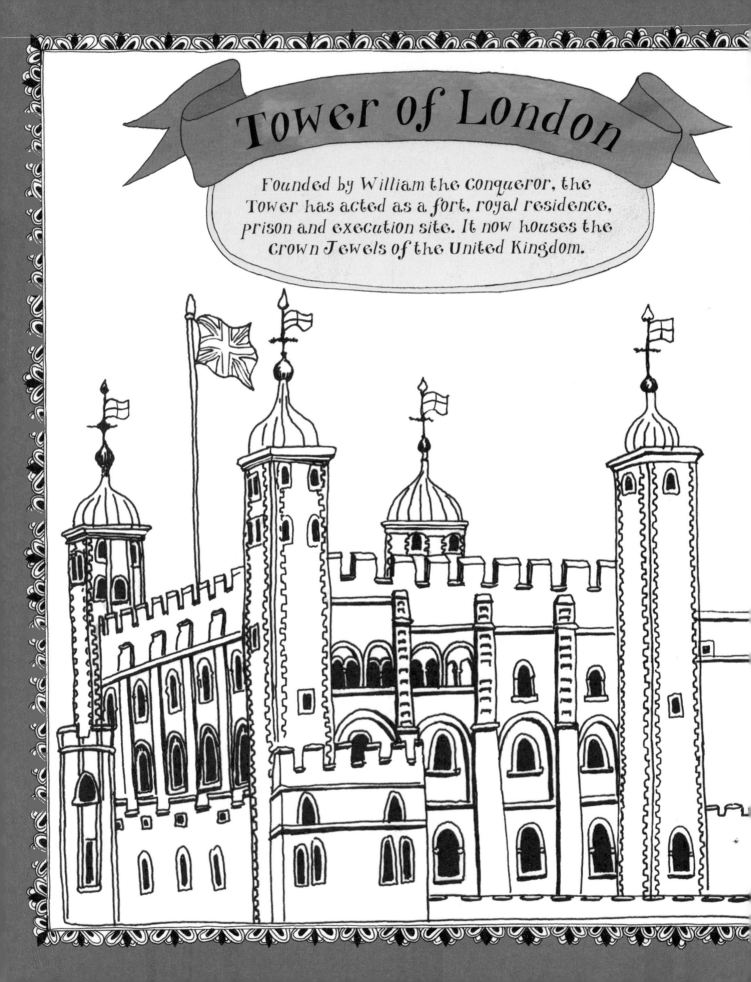

Tower of London

Founded by William the Conqueror, the Tower has acted as a fort, royal residence, prison and execution site. It now houses the Crown Jewels of the United Kingdom.

The Yeoman Warders, also known as Beefeaters, guard the Crown Jewels.

During World War Two, the Tower was used to secure prisoners of war. The last person to be executed there was a German spy, killed by firing squad in 1941.

Legend says that there must always be at least six ravens in residence at the Tower. If not, the kingdom will fall.

I'm one of the Tower's seven ravens (six plus a spare)!

Draw the Queen wearing her crown.

British Museum

The British Museum has a collection of over eight million artefacts. It displays items representing the span of human history, including ancient Egyptian mummies.

Draw your own Ming vase patterns using a blue pen or pencil.

The Ming dynasty ruled China for almost 300 years until 1644. The ceramics made during that time are extremely valuable.

The O2

The world's most popular music venue was built to celebrate the new millennium. Today it hosts music concerts and sporting competitions.

The O2 is famous for the exciting shows inside it – but it's pretty exciting outside too! Visitors can climb across the O2's roof with the help of a guide – it's not for the faint-hearted, but provides amazing city views.

Colour in the O2. Imagine it's covered in spectacular lights for a concert!

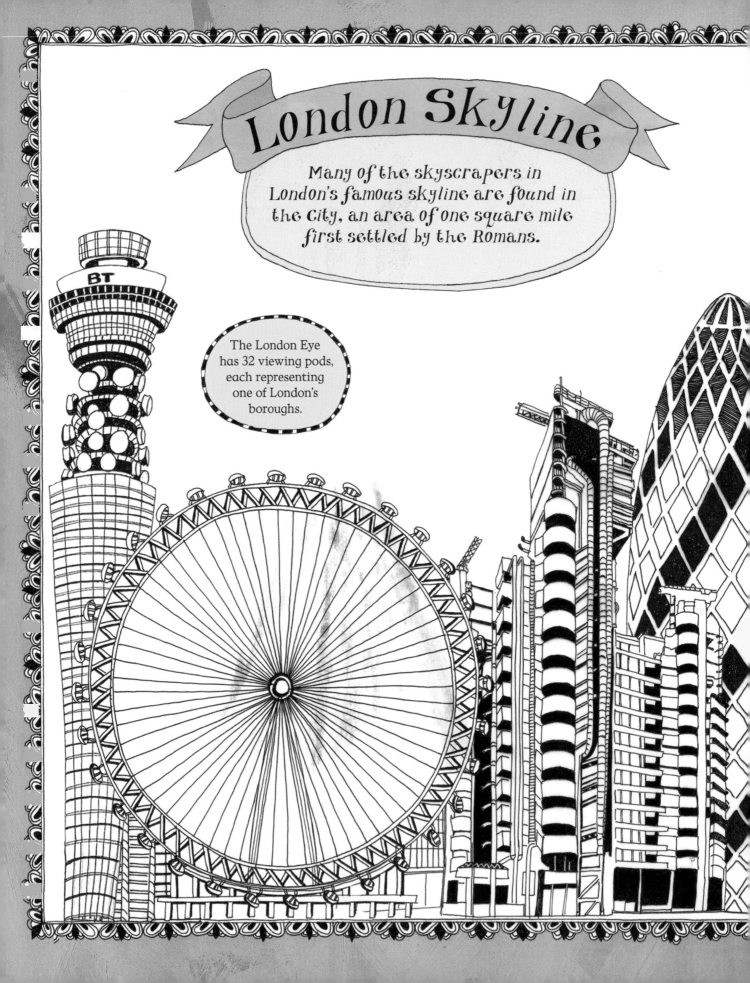

London Skyline

Many of the skyscrapers in London's famous skyline are found in the City, an area of one square mile first settled by the Romans.

The London Eye has 32 viewing pods, each representing one of London's boroughs.

BT

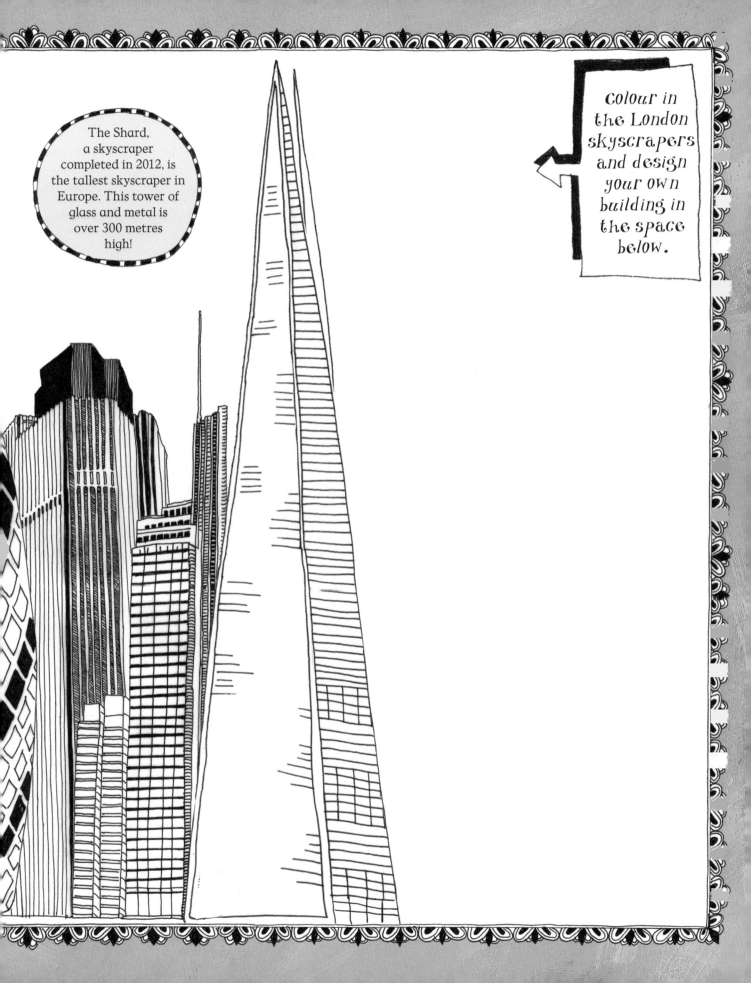

The Shard, a skyscraper completed in 2012, is the tallest skyscraper in Europe. This tower of glass and metal is over 300 metres high!

Colour in the London skyscrapers and design your own building in the space below.

The world
of
JENNIE
MAIZELS

ISBN 978-1-4063-2157-9

ISBN 978-1-4063-6427-9

ISBN 978-1-4063-4945-0

First published 2015 by Walker Books Ltd
87 Vauxhall Walk, London SE11 5HJ

2 4 6 8 10 9 7 5 3 1

Text © 2015 Walker Books Ltd. Illustrations © 2011 Jennie Maizels

The right of Jennie Maizels to be identified as illustrator of this work has been asserted by her in accordance
with the Copyright, Designs and Patents Act 1988

This book has been typeset in Veronan and hand-lettered by Jennie Maizels

Printed in China

British Library Cataloguing in Publication Data: a catalogue record for this book is available from the British Library

ISBN 978-1-4063-6426-2

www.walker.co.uk

Build Tower Bridge!

Tower Bridge is world famous for opening to allow tall ships to pass through. It opens about 850 times a year.

Side A

GLUE
(Side A)

GLUE
(Side A)

GLUE
(Side A)

Instructions

1. Tear out these card pages along the perforation lines, then colour in Tower Bridge.

2. Cut out the bridge pieces, following the dashed outlines of sides A and B.

3. Ask an adult to help you carefully cut along the 3 dashed lines of the inner rectangles on sides A and B – make sure you don't cut along the dotted line on the bottom.

4. On side A, make a fold away from you along the bottom of the inner rectangle, so it passes "through" the bridge. Repeat with side B.

5. Fold the bottom tabs of both sides away from you, "under" the bridge.

6. Glue the side A inner rectangle beneath the side B road, forming the bridge. Then glue the side B bottom tabs beneath the side A bottom tabs.

7. Admire your 3D model of Tower Bridge!

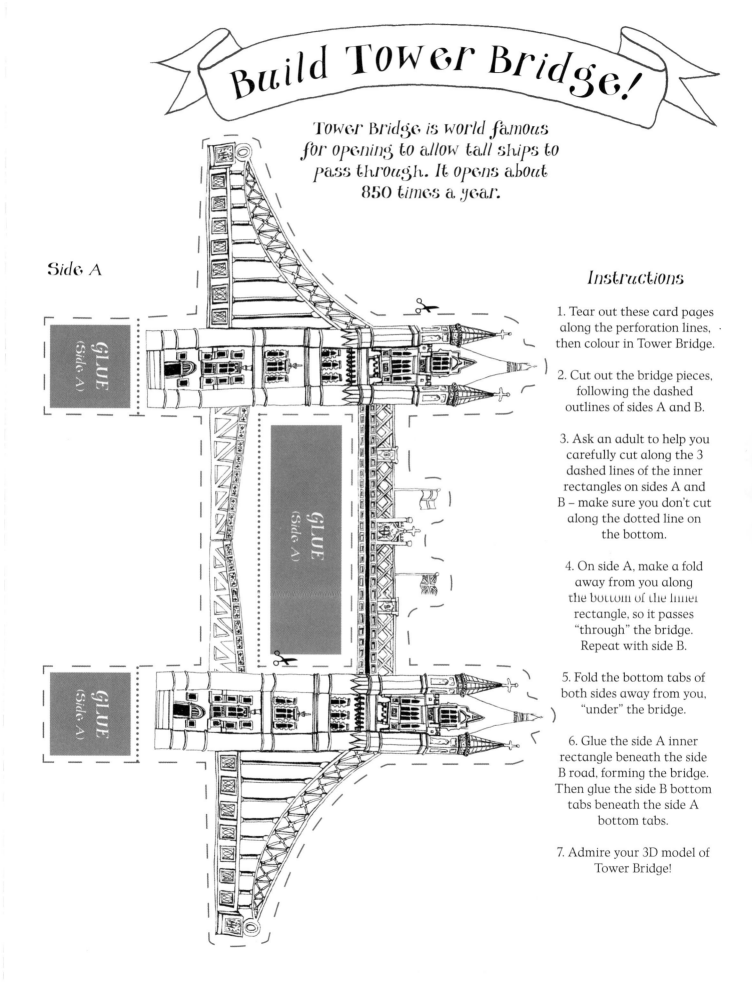

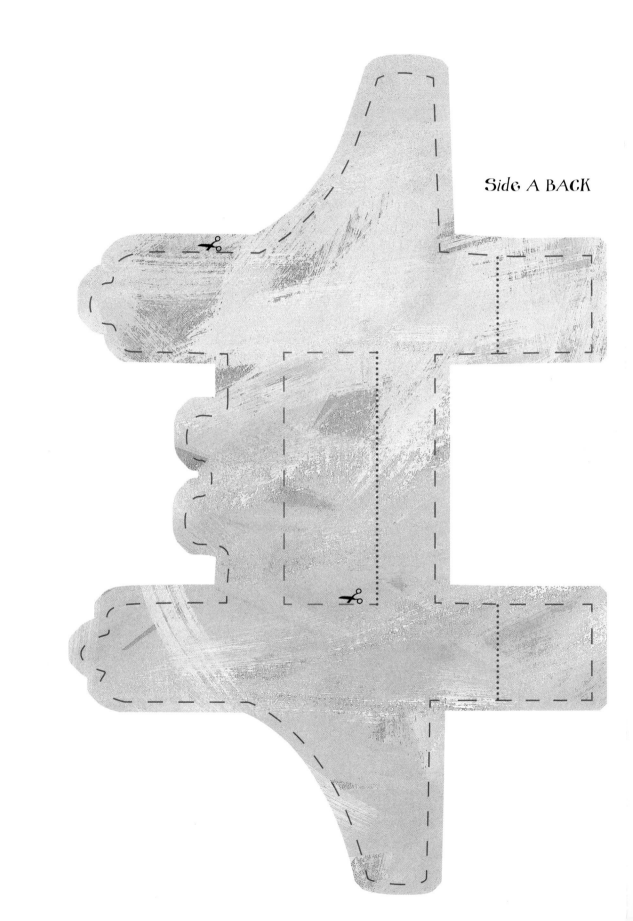

Side A BACK

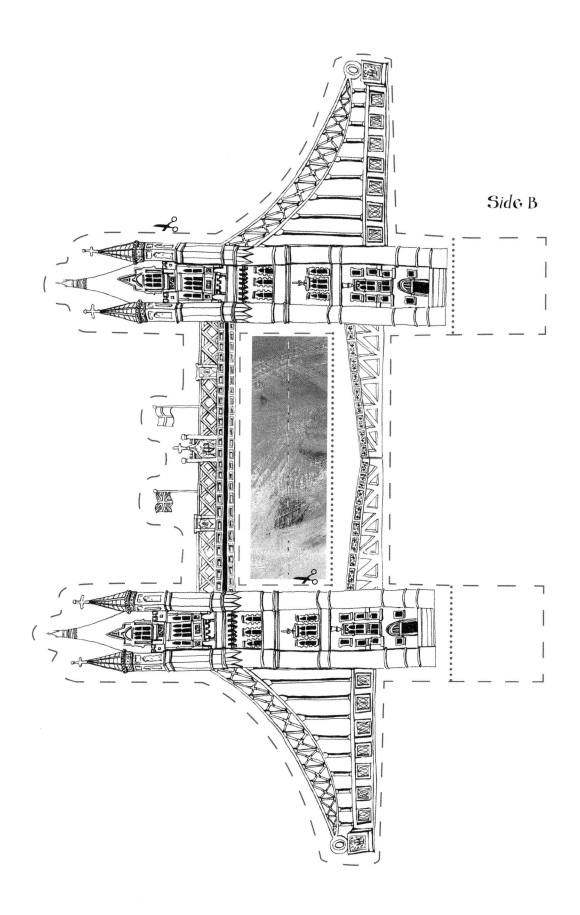

Side B

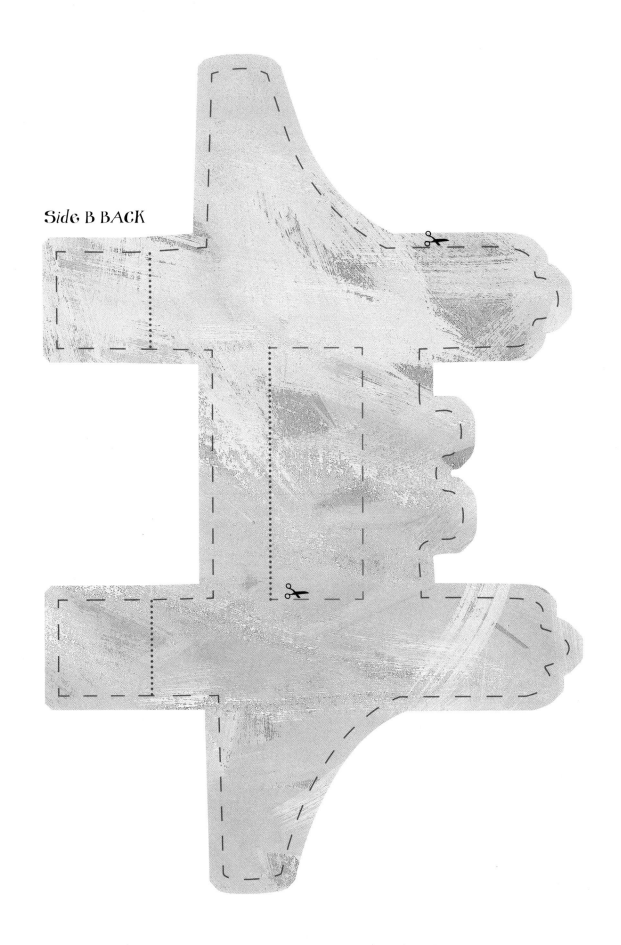

Side B BACK